Disney · PIXAR

SUPER COLOURING

Autumn Publishing

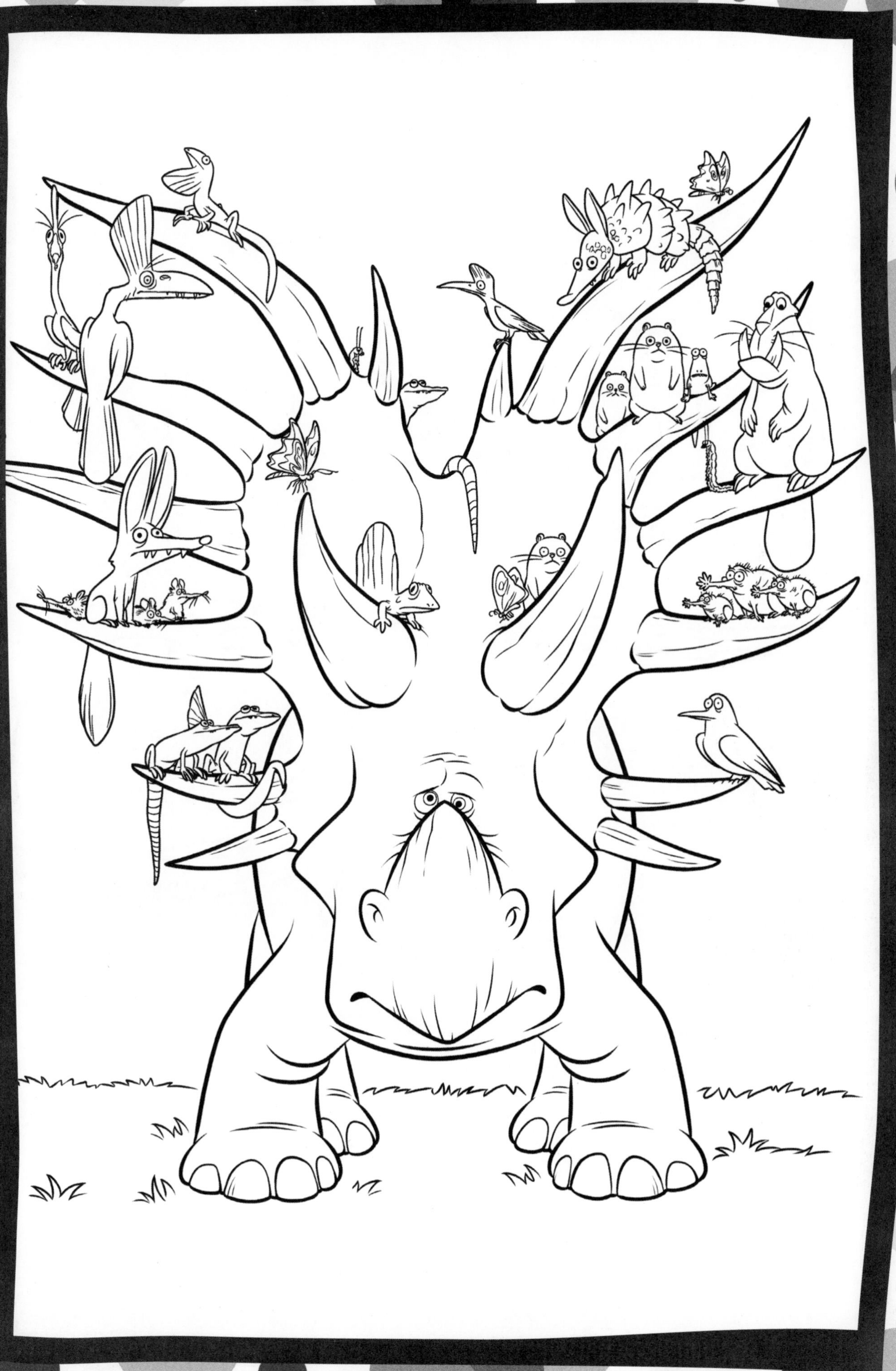

DINOCO
400
at ARIZONA
COPPER CANYON SPEEDWAY
Rust-eze
95
Medicated
Rust-eze
BUMPER OINTMENT
REAR END FORMULA
IGNTR
LIQUID ADRENALINE

DINOCO
DINOCO
DINOCO
DINOCO
51
51
95

Spirit
Of
Adventure

N
W
E
S

Woody's
ROUNDUP
AS SEEN ON
TV
PROSPEC

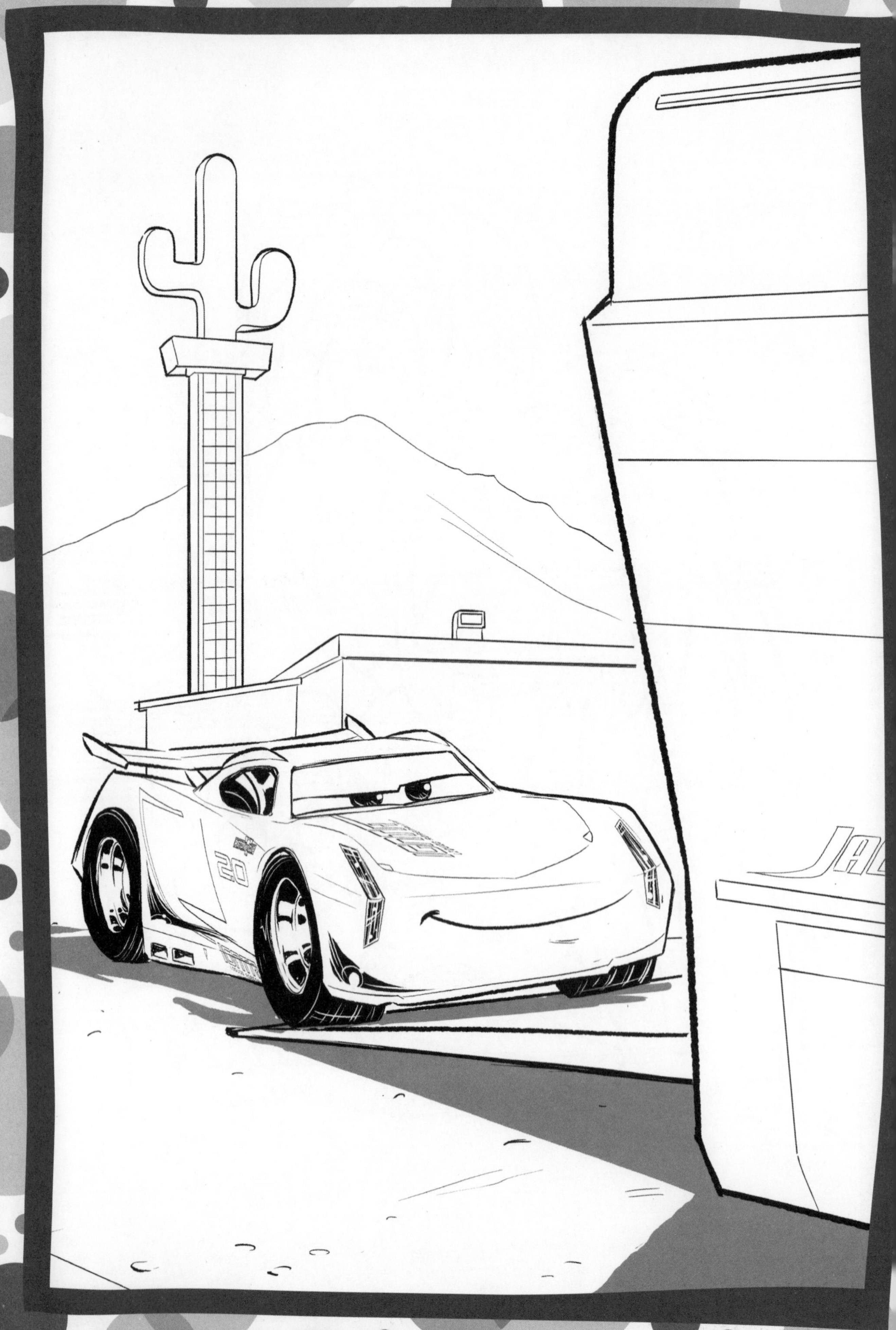

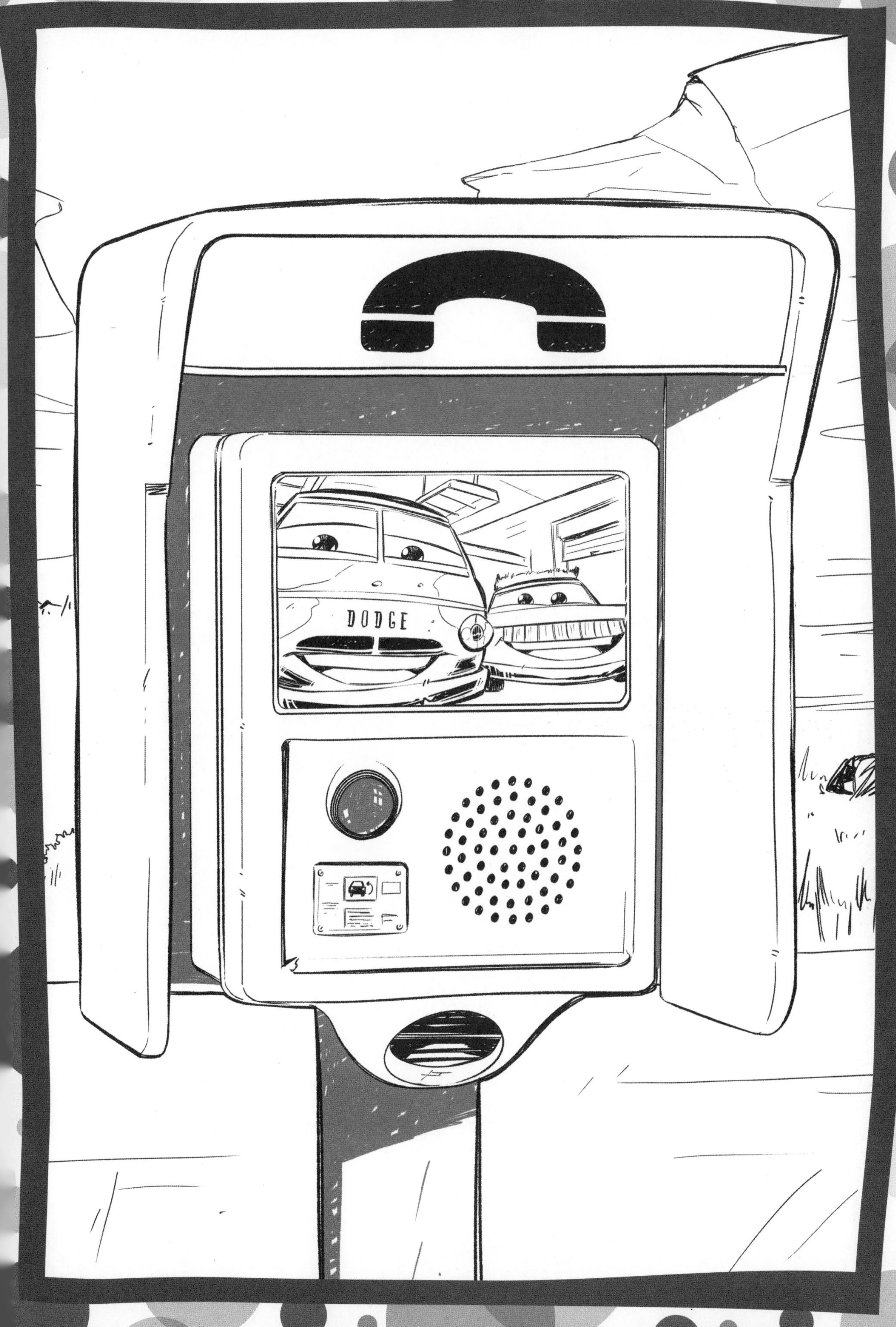
DODGE

OK
OK
OK

MU

Imagination
Land

THOMASVILLE
Home of 51
"The Fabulous Hudson Hornet"
SPEEDWAY
95